Mark Shark 2
Toby Glover©2023

Mark Shark came out of the sea.
He said HELLO! to you, then HELLO! to me.

Mark Shark went to your school.
He came to our school?
Wow! That is so super cool!

A shark in the school? That breaks all the rules!

MARK SHARK! GET OUT OF THIS SCHOOL!

Mark stayed in our school, where he wasn't allowed.

And all of us children, we showed him around.

We showed him our music room,
where he made such a din.

Shaking two tambourines in his great white fins.

A shark in the school? That breaks all the rules!

MARK SHARK! GET OUT OF THIS SCHOOL!

We showed him our blocks,
He built a tower to ten.

Then even to twenty!
Then right back again!

We showed him our playground,
He had so much fun,
ZOOM! ZOOM! ZOOM!
Like the Formula One!

A shark in the school? That breaks all the rules!

MARK SHARK! GET OUT OF THIS SCHOOL!

We showed him our garden, where he planted some seeds.

We showed him our book corner, where he sat for a read.

A shark in the school? That breaks all the rules!

MARK SHARK! GET OUT OF THIS SCHOOL!

We showed him our gym, where he got so much fitter.

We showed him our art room,
Oh no! Pens, glue and glitter!

A shark in the school? That breaks all the rules!

MARK SHARK! GET OUT OF THIS SCHOOL!

We showed him our workshop,
Where he built a train-set.

We showed him our role-play, where he loved our class pet...

VET'S

A shark in the school? That breaks all the rules!

MARK SHARK! GET OUT OF THIS SCHOOL!

Mark so loved our school, he so wanted to stay,
But was way too big, for our class water tray.

It was time to return, to the other sea creatures. But Mark felt a bit hungry...

So may I please eat your teachers?

A school without teachers,
Could be pretty sweet!

But how would we learn?
If we let him go eat...

So we hugged him goodbye,
Mark went on his way.
We will never forget,
Such a super cool day!

So Mark Shark went back to the sea.
He said GOODBYE! to you, then GOODBYE! to me.

Mark's all tired and sleepy, on his seabed so blue.
He said GOODNIGHT to me, then GOODNIGHT to you.

fin

How many do you have...?

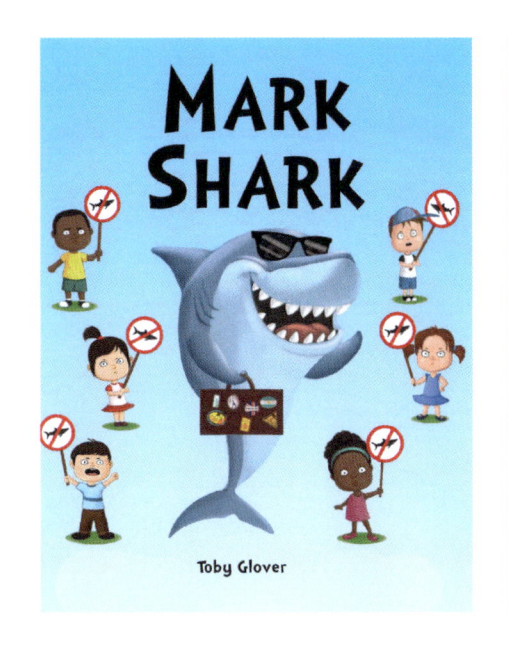

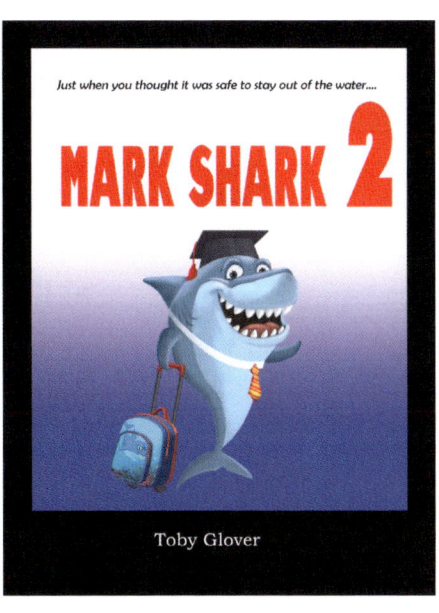

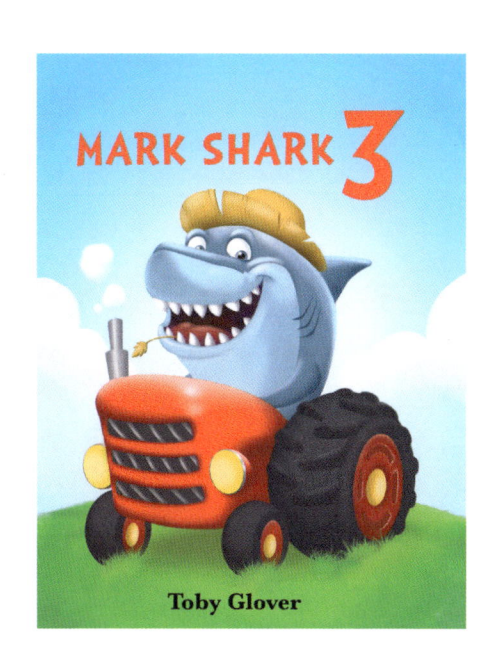

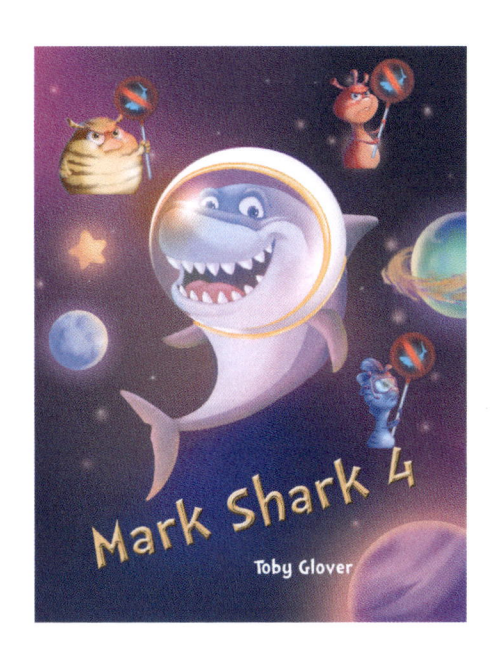

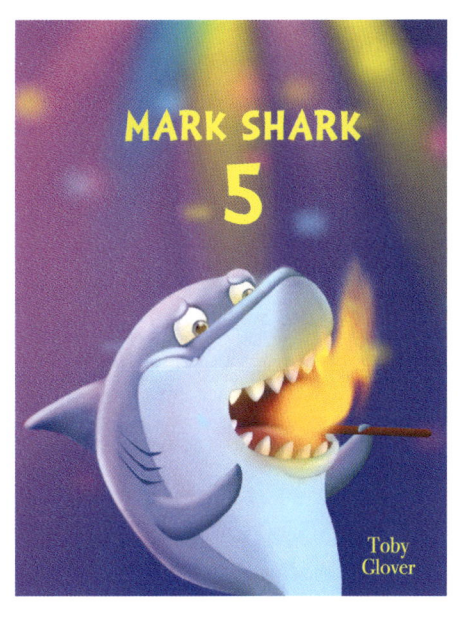

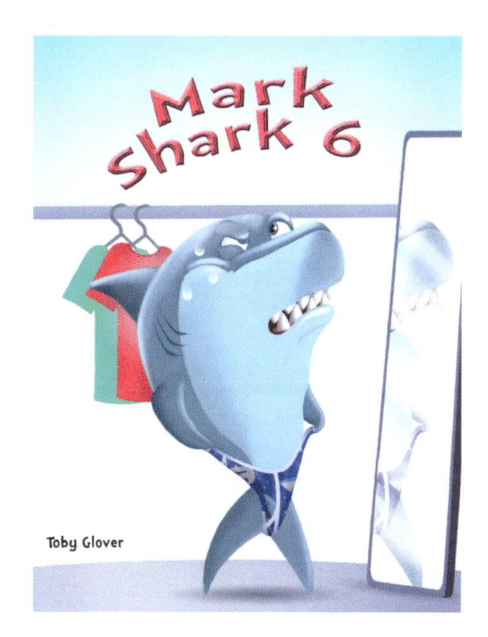

To hear more of Toby's stories scan the QR code...

Printed in Great Britain
by Amazon